Ready to Stitch
Borders & Motifs

Michaela Learner

SEARCHPRESS

First published in 2014

Search Press Limited
Wellwood, North Farm Road,
Tunbridge Wells, Kent TN2 3DR

Illustrations on pages 9–13 by Bess Harding

Photographs by Paul Bricknell at Search Press Studio

ISBN: 978-1-84448-909-1

Suppliers

All of the threads used in the book were kindly supplied by DMC Creative World. Visit www.dmc.com for details of nearest stockist. If you have any difficulty obtaining any of the materials and equipment mentioned in this book, please visit the Search Press website: www.searchpress.com

Publishers' notes

All the embroideries in this book were made by the author, Michaela Learner, using threads supplied by DMC.

Please note: to remove the transfers of the borders and motifs you want to use from the book, cut round them carefully. They can be stored in the pocket at the back of the book and used several times.

Printed in China

The images used in this book were previously published by Search Press in:

Design Source Books:

Celtic Borders & Motifs by Lesley Davies, 2005

Tudor Designs by Polly Pinder, 2005

Classic Border Designs by Judy Balchin, 2004

Floral Borders & Motifs by Penny Brown, 2005

Oriental Flower Designs by Polly Pinder, 2004

Art Nouveau Borders & Motifs by Judy Balchin, 2005

The Design Library:

Hearts & Flower Designs by Judy Balchin, 2012

and *The Complete Book of Fantasy Designs*, 2012

Dedication

This book is dedicated to the wonderful and enduring memory of my brother, Daniel Pugh, who shared with me his passion for books, giving me the ability to be one of life's dreamers.

Acknowledgements

My sincere thanks to all those who helped make this book possible. These include DMC for all the threads, Zweigart for the sampler fabrics, Framecraft for the cards and Beads Unlimited for all the beads. I'd also like to thank my mother, Ann Miles and my mother-in-law, Patricia Learner, for the noble sacrifice of their best linens to a good cause, and finally a big thanks to my husband, Chaz, for never complaining about losing the living room under an ever growing mountain of craft supplies!

Contents

Introduction

For as long as people have been wearing clothes, there has been decorative hand embroidery in one form or another. The basic stitches have changed very little over the centuries but there has been an exciting explosion of thread and fabric types in more recent times.

This book has been arranged around a core of 32 designs, although by picking and choosing elements from within the designs, the number of available ideas could be far greater. Only ten easy to learn stitches have been used to create all the decorative embroidery you see here. Instructions and advice are given on choosing and setting up your fabrics ready for stitching, how to use an embroidery hoop and which threads suit your ideas best. The samplers are shown on pages 16–81, with keys showing which threads, colours and stitches were used, in case you want to reproduce them exactly.

At the back of the book are all the transfers, so that the designs for the samplers can be ironed on to the fabric, with full instructions available on page 14.

The projects on pages 82–95 have been included to give you some inspiration, showing what can be created very easily in a couple of evenings using the border and motifs in this book. Or you may choose to combine several of the transfers into a different design such as that shown on the contents page.

Take your time and enjoy the process as well as the final result and you will be creating your own heirloom pieces in no time.

What you need

Very little is needed to start embroidery – just some fabric, thread, a needle, pins, an embroidery hoop and a pair of scissors. Once you have these to hand and you have chosen a design, now comes the fun bit: you get to pick threads and fabrics from the wonderful array available.

Fabric

The most suitable fabrics for use with the transfers are cotton or cotton/linen blends. They take the transfers well and hold their shape while being stitched. However, it is not always possible to choose your fabric, for example when stitching an item of clothing, so it is always best to do a small test with the transfer on an inconspicuous corner or edge, to determine suitability.

The fabric I used for the samplers in this book was Zweigart Normandy 3442, which is available in white, cream and natural. It is a cotton/linen mix which is washable up to 60°C and has a good body and resistance to puckering when you work, although it is always advisable to support your stitching with a hoop or frame to ensure smooth results.

Thread

As far as decorative thread is concerned, if you can imagine stitching with it, you probably can! Traditionally, stranded cottons and silks as well as crewel wool were used, and these are probably the easiest solution.

When stitching the samplers in this book, I used DMC threads throughout. They come in a great array of shades and types, as you will see from the samplers, and are always colourfast. The keys to the samplers show you exactly which types and shades were used in each design. You can of course make your own choices from the wonderful range available, or use another range if you prefer.

If you are a confident embroiderer and decide to push the boundaries a bit, some stunning results can be achieved. Try using crochet cotton, cotton perle, dressmaking threads, or even strips of plastic bags or hessian threads removed from a piece of sacking.

Equipment

The basic items of equipment required are a selection of embroidery needles in different sizes, embroidery scissors, pins to hold your transfer, an iron and a suitable embroidery hoop or frame. You may also want to consider a natural light lamp to prevent eye strain and enable good colour selection from the range of threads.

Stitches used

Ten simple embroidery stitches have been used to produce all of the designs in this book. Don't be afraid to experiment and try different combinations of stitches, thread colours and fabrics – you will be amazed by their versatility and the wonderful effects you can achieve.

Starting to stitch

Bring your needle and thread up through the fabric on the spot where you are going to place your first stitch. You will need to hold the end of the thread to stop it going right through (1). Make sure your first three or four stitches go over the starting thread on the wrong side of the fabric to secure it (2).

Alternatively, make a small knot at the end of your thread and insert the needle down into the fabric about 2.5cm (1in) away from where your first stitch will be placed. It must be along the line of your first few stitches. Bring the needle up where you are going to start stitching (3). Embroider the first few stitches up to the knot, making sure you have stitched over the starting thread on the back of your work. You can now snip off the knot and continue stitching (4).

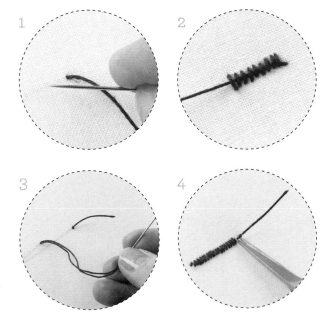

Fastening off a thread

To fasten off a thread, slip the needle through the back of the stitches you have just worked (5), pull the thread through and snip off the tail (6). To rejoin a thread, slip the thread through the back of the same stitches and continue stitching.

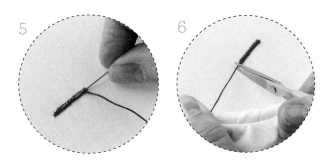

Straight stitch

Straight stitch is the simplest of all the stitches and is great for adding little details. This stitch can be used to add subtle shading to the centre of a flower, as in the flowers in sampler 16, or it can be used to create fine details like the fish scales in sampler 21.

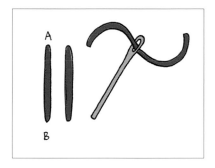

Bring the needle up at A and insert it at B to create a single, long stitch. Make further stitches as required.

Back stitch

Back stitch is the real workhorse of the embroidery world. It is perfect for outlining small detailed areas such as the pixie faces in sampler 31. Alternatively, it can be used as a stand-alone single stitch to complete an entire piece of work. This works particularly well when combined with a multicoloured thread, as shown on the pale butterfly border in sampler 7.

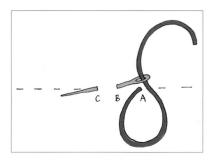
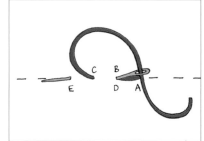
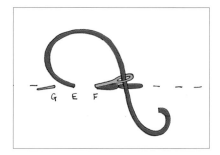

1 Bring the needle up at A and pull the thread through. Insert the needle at B and bring it through at C. Pull the thread through the fabric.

2 Insert the needle at D and bring it up at E. Pull the thread through.

3 Insert the needle at F and bring it up at G. Continue working along the stitch line until it is completed. To finish off, thread your needle through the stitches on the wrong side of your work.

Chain stitch

Chain stitch is one of the most versatile of the stitches. As an outlining stitch it is just perfect, as can be seen on the Christmas tree in sampler 29. A less common but equally effective use can be as a filling stitch, worked either in rows or circles, as shown on the wings of the butterflies in sampler 7.

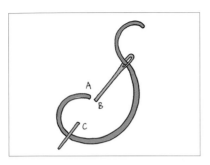

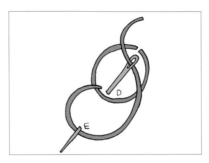

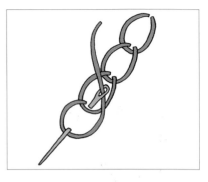

1 Bring the needle up through the fabric at A and pull the thread through. Insert the needle at B, as close as possible to A, and bring it up at C. Keep the thread under the needle. Pull the thread through gently to form the first chain.

2 Insert the needle at D, as close as possible to C, and bring the needle up at E. Keeping the thread under the needle, pull the thread through gently to form the second chain.

3 Continue in this way, making evenly sized chain stitches, until the line of stitching is complete.

French knots

French knots, although a little fiddly to learn, are well worth the effort as they have many uses. A single stitch can be used to create a specific detail such as an eye or a flower centre (see sampler 32), or group them together and they can be used to fill a larger area such as the floral centre in sampler 25.

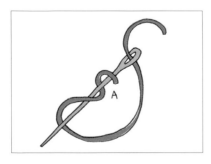

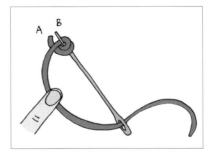

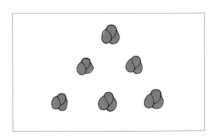

1 Bring the thread through where the knot is required, at A. Holding the thread between your thumb and finger, wrap it around the needle twice.

2 Hold the thread firmly with your thumb and turn the needle back to A. Insert it as close to A as possible, at B, and pull the thread through to form a knot.

3 Make as many knots as you need. Make a small stitch on the wrong side of the fabric before fastening off.

Lazy daisy (detached chain) stitch

Lazy daisy is an easy little stitch that packs a punch. Use it to create flower petals on smaller designs like the flowers in sampler 32. A less common application is as a spot filling. Just group some daisy stitches together and then repeat over an area, as on the body of the sleeping pixie on sampler 31.

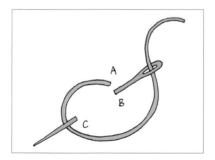

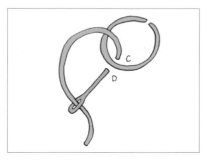

1 Bring the thread through at A and, securing the thread with your thumb, insert the needle at B, as close to A as possible. Bring the needle through at C. Pull the thread through gently to create a loop.

2 Insert the needle at D, making sure you pass the thread over the loop, to secure.

3 Make as many stitches as required, then make a small stitch on the wrong side of your work to secure.

Blanket stitch

Blanket stitch is another of those underrated stitches. Most commonly used as an edging stitch, it can, however, create an amazing filled cord effect if you work two interlocking rows as shown on the motif in sampler 1. In sampler 6, a lovely delicate edge has be formed using just a couple of stitches.

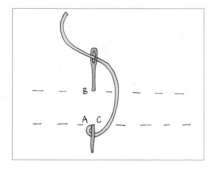

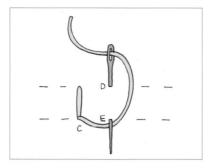

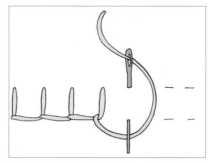

1 Bring the needle up through the fabric at A and pull the thread through. Take it back down at B and up at C, as close as possible to A. Take care to keep the thread under the needle. Use your thumb to secure the thread. Pull the thread through gently to form the first stitch.

2 Leaving the required space between stitches, insert the needle at D and come up at E, keeping the thread under the needle while pulling the thread through.

3 Repeat steps 1 and 2. Try not to pull the stitches too tightly as this can cause the stitch to distort and the fabric to pucker. To finish, make a small stitch to the right of the final loop, take the thread to the wrong side of the fabric and fasten off.

Seed stitch

This is a great little stitch. Work it sparsely to give a light shading effect, an example of which can be found in the leaves of sampler 4. Alternatively, just go for it and work loads of overlapping stitches for a great filling, like the frame in sampler 3.

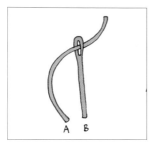

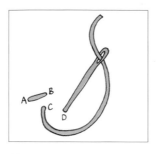

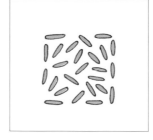

1 Bring the needle up at A and insert it at B to create a tiny stitch.

2 Bring the needle up at C and insert it at D to make a second stitch at a different angle.

3 Continue placing the stitches randomly until the area is filled.

Long and short stitch

Long and short stitch is perfect for filling in larger areas, particularly where a shaded effect is required. You can vary the effect with the number of threads used. A great example of single thread long and short stitch shading can be found in sampler 16, on the petals and leaves.

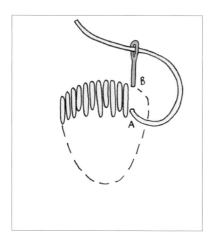

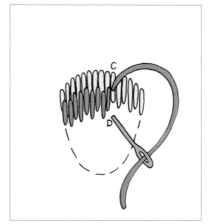

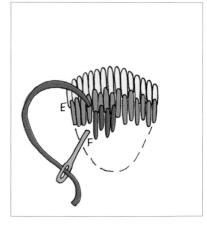

1 Work from the middle of the outer edge of the shape to be filled and move outwards, then come back to the middle and work the other side of the shape. Bring the needle out at A and in at B. Repeat to fill the top edge.

2 Work subsequent rows as before but this time bring the needle out through the stitches at C and in at D. This will ensure a nice, flat surface, free of little holes. Each stitch does not have to be split; sometimes it will be necessary to come up between stitches to give a neat, even fill to the shape.

3 Continue for the next row, coming out at E and in at F, until your shape is completely filled. Remember to vary the stitch lengths to give a smooth, blended finish.

Satin stitch

Satin stitch is good for filling smaller areas quickly. The stitches look best worked closely together and the effect can be particularly pleasing if a multicoloured thread is used, like the brown in sampler 20.

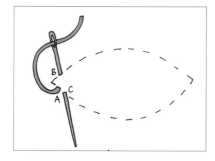

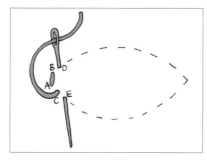

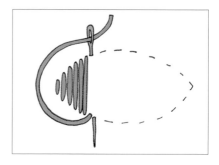

1 Bring your thread up at A, on the edge of the shape, and insert the needle at B. Pull the thread through gently. Pulling the thread too tightly will cause the fabric to pucker. Bring the needle up at C working as close to A as possible.

2 Take the needle down at D, as close as possible to B, and bring it back through at E, next to C. Pull the thread through gently to make a stitch that lies next to the first stitch, without overlapping it.

3 Continue as above until the shape is filled. Pass the needle through to the back of the work to fasten off.

Stem stitch

Stem stitch makes a lovely smooth, unbroken line. This can be used to create stems like those in sampler 9. A more imaginative use can be as a filling stitch, as in the hearts on the left of sampler 19, where a lovely shaded effect has been created using a darker thread for the outer edge.

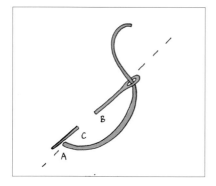

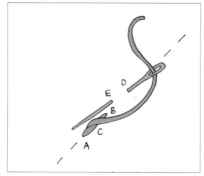

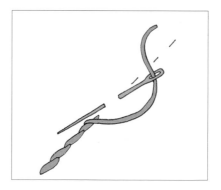

1 Bring the thread through at A and hold it down with your thumb to form a loop. Insert the needle at B and bring it out at C, between A and B.

2 Pull the thread through to make the first stitch. Hold the working thread down with your thumb as before. Insert the needle at D and bring it out at E, slightly to the side of B.

3 Continue until the line of stitching is complete. If using as a filling stitch, simply work another row next to the first and repeat until the area is filled.

Transferring the designs

The transfer sheets for all the designs are at the back of this book. You can cut around the parts you want to use individually, but make sure you leave as much paper as possible around the edge. When you have used the transfer, store it in the pocket on the back cover to keep it safe until you wish to use it again. Transfer the designs using an ordinary iron (without steam) set on 'cotton'. Make sure you use a fabric that is not damaged by this heat. If possible, use a spare piece of your fabric to check before you start.

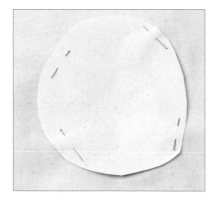

1 Pin the transfer ink-side down on the right side of the fabric where you want the design to be.

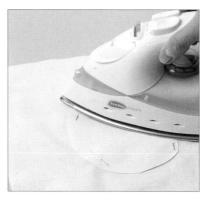

2 Place the iron over the transfer area and leave for about ten seconds. Do not move the iron, as this may blur the image. Carefully lift a corner of the transfer to make sure it has printed on to the fabric. If not, leave the iron for a little longer or increase the temperature and try again.

3 When you are happy that the design has transferred successfully, remove the transfer. Your design is now ready to be placed in the embroidery hoop for stitching.

Using dark and heavily patterned fabrics

If your fabric is dark or has a heavy all-over pattern, this will make it hard to see the transferred outline. To overcome this problem you can embroider the design on to a piece of plain or lighter-coloured fabric and then sew it on to the darker fabric. Alternatively, the transfer can be ironed on to a water-soluble fabric. This can then be tacked on to the item to be stitched and washed away when the stitching has been completed.

Using an embroidery hoop

If you decide to use an embroidery hoop, make sure it is large enough to include the whole of the design within the frame, but not so large that there is insufficient fabric around the outside to secure it. Binding the inner hoop will not only help to hold the fabric more firmly but also avoid the frame marking the fabric. Use a woven tape 2.5cm (1in) wide.

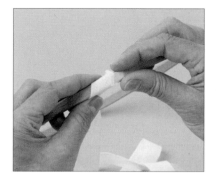

1 Tape the end of the binding at a 45° angle. Secure the end by using a little piece of masking tape.

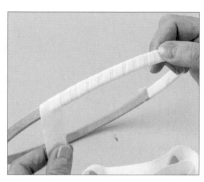

2 Wrap the tape around the hoop with one hand whilst using your thumb on the other hand to keep the tape secure. You need to pull the tape fairly tight to stop it sagging or any gaps appearing.

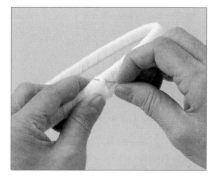

3 When you reach the end, remove the masking tape and wrap the remaining tape over the gap and a couple more to make sure the ends overlap. Stitch the ends together and trim off any surplus.

4 Lay the bound inner hoop on a firm surface. Place the fabric over the hoop with the design facing upwards. Keeping the tension screw at the top, put the outer ring over the top and press down to sandwich the fabric between the inner and outer hoops.

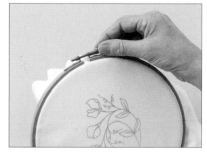

5 Tighten the tension screw (a small screwdriver is sometimes useful here).

6 Holding the hoop in one hand, gently ease out any slack in the fabric. The fabric should now be nice and tight in the frame.

The samplers

The following stitched samplers give just one idea for stitching each of the transfers. Each of the samplers has a number which corresponds with a transfer at the back of the book for ease of identification.

This is not a strict 'how to' section, so if you want to change stitches or threads, feel free to let your imagination be your guide and simply let these samplers inspire you. You may wish to stitch only a specific part of a design rather than the whole image, in which case just trim the transfer to suit your requirements.

If you want to stitch these samplers exactly as I have done, follow the key on the facing page, which gives the DMC colours used, and the stitches and threads used in each part of the design.

If you decide to get creative, let the fabric be your guide in terms of shades and stitches used. For example you would not want to use heavy filling stitches on a very lightweight fabric. When stitching a larger piece, it may be useful to work a small sample on a scrap of waste fabric to check if your colour and stitch choices are working together well.

Getting started

Once you have selected your design, transfer it to your fabric (see page 14) and secure it in an embroidery hoop (see page 15). You are then ready to start. Begin by gathering together the tools and threads you need (see pages 6–7), then select which stitch you want to start with. Start in the centre of the design and work outwards, as this will give a neater finish. Follow the printed lines closely and make sure they are covered as much as possible by the stitching. Although they will fade with washing, they may not disappear completely.

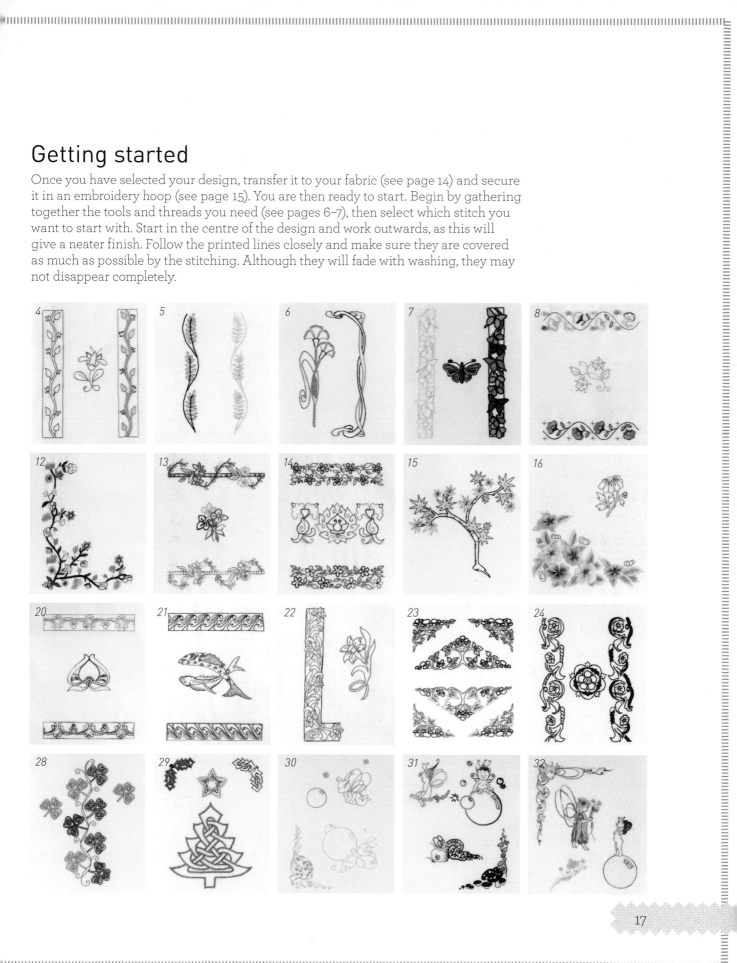

1

Thread key

DMC colours used:

- 913
- 946
- 333
- 349
- 743
- 334

Stitches and threads used for central flower:

Use 2 strands throughout.

Central ring worked in stem stitch with 743.

Outer blue petals worked in two interlacing rows of blanket stitch with 334.

Red petals worked in two interlacing rows of blanket stitch with 349.

Central yellow petals worked in two interlacing rows of blanket stitch with 743.

Leaves between petals worked in satin stitch in 913, 333 and 946.

Mini petals around red and yellow petals worked in lazy daisy stitch with 333 and 946.

Flower centre worked in overlaid seed stitches in 743, 946, 349 and 333.

Stitches and threads used for left-hand border:

Use 2 strands throughout.

Leaves worked in stem stitch with 913.

Orange details in flowers worked in lazy daisy stitch with 946.

Flowers worked in satin stitch with 333.

Hearts worked in satin stitch with 349.

Stems worked in satin stitch with 913.

Stitch and thread used for right-hand border:

All worked with 2 strands of 333 in back stitch.

2

Thread key

DMC colours used:

■	4210 colour variations
■	603 and 30603 rayon
■	988 and 30367 rayon
■	208 and 30550 rayon

Stitches and threads used for left-hand border:

■ Petals worked in satin stitch with 2 strands of 4210 colour variations.

■ Pink stems worked in stem stitch using 1 strand each, combined, of 603 and 30603 rayon.

■ Main green stem and leaves worked in long and short stitch using 1 strand each, combined, of 988 and 30367 rayon.

■ Purple flower bases worked in long and short stitch using 1 strand each, combined, of 208 and 30550 rayon.

Stitches and threads used for right-hand border:

■ Purple flower bases worked in back stitch using 1 strand each, combined, of 208 and 30550 rayon.

■ Green stems and leaves worked in stem stitch using 1 strand each, combined, of 988 and 30367 rayon.

■ Petals worked in stem stitch using 2 strands of 4210 colour variations.

■ Pink stems worked in back stitch using 1 strand each, combined of 603 and 30603 rayon.

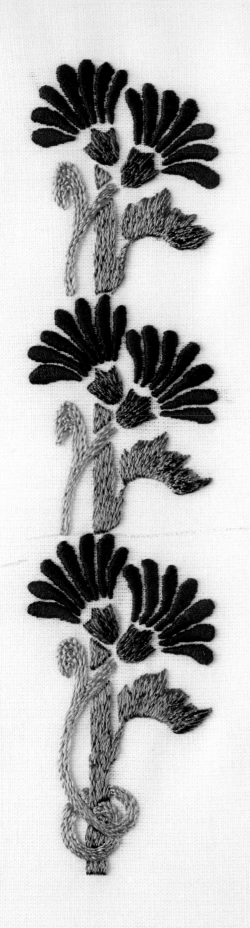

3

Thread key

DMC colours used:

E3852 precious metals

3824

4120 colour variations

3340

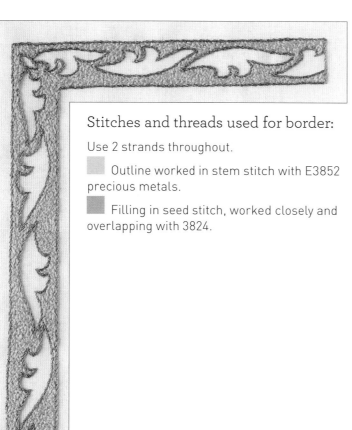

Stitches and threads used for border:

Use 2 strands throughout.

Outline worked in stem stitch with E3852 precious metals.

Filling in seed stitch, worked closely and overlapping with 3824.

Stitches and threads used for flower motif:

Use 2 strands throughout.

Flower outlines worked in back stitch with 4120 colour variations.

Stem outline worked in back stitch with 3340.

Flower centres worked in French knots with 4120 colour variations.

4

Thread key

DMC colours used:

- 334
- 913
- 3766

Stitch and thread used for left-hand border:

Use 2 strands throughout.

Outline worked in back stitch with 334.

Stitches and threads used for flower motif:

Use 2 strands throughout.

Green stem and leaf midribs worked in stem stitch in 913.

Blue calyx and leaf outlines worked in back stitch in 334.

Stamens worked in back stitch in 3766.

Upright petals worked in chain stitch in 334.

Upright green flower centre worked in chain stitch in 913.

Bent over petals worked in chain stitch in 3766.

Stitches and threads used for right-hand border:

Use 2 strands throughout.

Green outlines worked in stem stitch in 913.

Stem filled with stem stitch worked in rows, in 3766.

Leaves filled with seed stitch in 3766.

Beads:

2 per circle, rainbow rocailles.

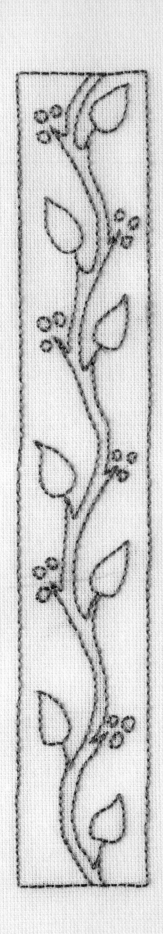

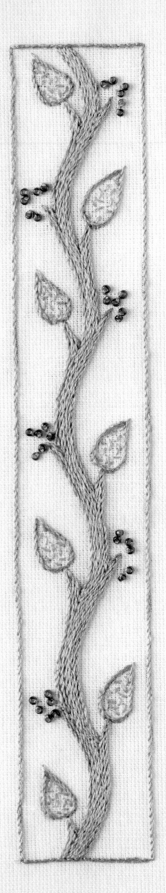

5

Thread key

DMC colours used:

 E898 light effects

E436 light effects

4100 colour variations

Stitches and threads used for left-hand border:

Use 2 strands of light effects throughout.

■ Stem worked in stem stitch with E898.

■ Ears worked in lazy daisy stitch with E436.

Stitches and thread used for right-hand border:

Use 2 strands of colour variations throughout.

□ Stem worked in stem stitch and ears worked in lazy daisy stitch with 4100 colour variations.

6

Thread key

DMC colours used:

	3833
	355
	471

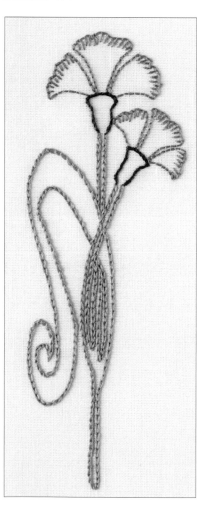

Stitches and threads used for flower motif:

Use 2 strands throughout.

Petal outlines worked in back stitch with 3833.

Petal edging worked in blanket stitch with 3833.

Calices worked in stem stitch with 355.

Stem and leaf worked in chain stitch with 471.

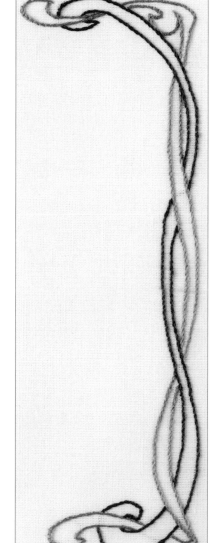

Stitches and threads used for border:

Use 2 strands throughout.

Border element from top left to bottom left worked in stem stitch with 3833.

Other intertwined border element worked in stem stitch with 355.

7

Thread key

DMC colours used:

- 4090 colour variations
- 310
- 601
- 970
- 741
- 3805
- 700
- 906
- 704
- 3844
- 3846

Stitches and threads used for butterfly motif:

Use 2 strands throughout.

Black outlines and antennae worked in stem stitch with 310.

Turquoise areas in top wings worked in satin stitch with 3844.

Pink areas in top wings worked in satin stitch with 601.

Body worked in satin stitch with 700.

Orange areas of lower wings worked in satin stitch with 970.

Green areas of top wings worked in stem stitch in rows with 704.

Turquoise areas of lower wings worked in stem stitch with 3846.

Stitch and thread used for left-hand border:

Use 2 strands throughout.

Border and butterfly outlines all worked in back stitch with 4090 colour variations

Stitches and threads used for right-hand border:

Use 2 strands throughout.

Black outlines worked in stem stitch with 310.

Butterfly wings worked in chain stitch with a darker row round the edge (0) and a fill colour (I): 3844 (0) and 3846 (I).

906 (0) and 704 (I).

601 (0) and 3805 (I).

970 (1) and 741 (I).

Butterfly bodies and main stem worked in stem stitch in rows with 310 and 700.

8

Thread key

DMC colours used:

- 604
- 211
- 3811
- 721
- 743
- 165

Stitches and threads used for flower motif:

Use 2 strands throughout.

Petals worked in long and short stitch with 604.

Leaf edges worked in blanket stitch with 211.

Flower centres and stems worked in stem stitch with 743, 165 and 3811.

Lines radiating from flower centres worked in straight stitch with 743.

Flower centres worked in French knots with 743.

Beads:

Use opaque yellow seed beads.

Stitches and threads used for top border:

Use 2 strands throughout.

Pink wavy stem worked in chain stitch with 604.

Petal edges worked in blanket stitch with 211, 721, 743 and 3811.

Calices and centres worked in satin stitch with 211, 165, 721, 743 and 3811.

Leaf outlines worked in stem stitch with 165, 211, 721 and 3811.

Leaves filled with lazy daisy stitch in 165, 721, 743 and 3811.

Flower stems worked in back stitch with 165, 721, 743 and 3811.

Beads:

Attach small floral beads using a seed bead at the centre.

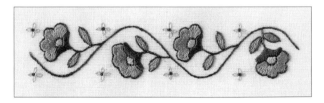

Stitches and threads used for bottom border:

Use 2 strands throughout.

Flowers and leaves filled with satin stitch with 211, 604 and 721.

Stem and flower outlines worked in stem stitch with 721.

Flower centres outlined in back stitch with 721.

Tiny flower petals worked in lazy daisy stitch with 211; centres are French knots with 721.

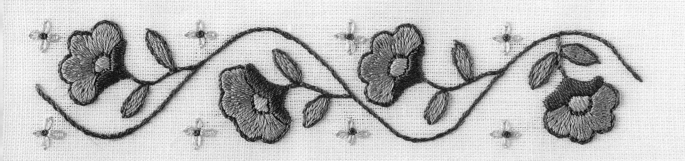

9

Thread key

DMC colours used:

- E130 jewel effects
- E718 jewel effects
- 326
- E321 jewel effects
- 956
- 4050 colour variations
- E699 jewel effects

Stitches and threads used for top border:

Use 2 strands of jewel effects throughout.

All stitched in back stitch with E130, E321, E699 and E718.

Stitch and threads used for flower motif:

Use 2 strands of jewel effects throughout.

All stitched in back stitch with E321 and E699.

Stitches and threads used for bottom border:

Use 2 strands throughout.

- Flower petals outlined in back stitch with 956.
- Stems worked in stem stitch with 326.
- Curled leaves outlined in stem stitch with 4050 colour variations.
- Inner flower shapes worked in satin stitch with 326.
- Buds worked in satin stitch with 956.
- Straight leaves worked in satin stitch with 4050 colour variations.
- Curled leaves filled with seed stitch with 4050 colour variations.

10

Thread key

DMC colours used:

 334

341

208

211

4020 colour variations

4030 colour variations

911

598

Stitches and threads used for top border:

Use 2 strands throughout.

Purple petals and buds worked in satin stitch with 208.

Blue petals and bud insides worked in satin stitch with 334.

Leaves worked in satin stitch with 4030 colour variations.

Stems worked in chain stitch with 911.

Beads for flower centres:

Tiny purple seed beads.

Stitches and threads used for flower motif:

Use 2 strands throughout.

Whole motif worked in chain stitch with 211, 208, 911, 4030 colour variations and 4020 colour variations.

Stitches and threads used for bottom border:

Use 2 strands throughout.

Pale purple petals and buds worked in satin stitch with 211.

Purple petals and bud insides worked in satin stitch with 341.

Leaves worked in satin stitch with 4020 colour variations.

Stems worked in chain stitch with 598.

Beads for flower centres:

Tiny pale assorted seed beads.

Thread key

DMC colours used:

■	666		■	368
■	208		■	3346
■	211		■	310
■	743		■	498
■	907			

Stitches and threads used:

Use 2 strands throughout.

■ The darker purple in the irises is worked in long and short stitch with 208.

■ The paler purple in the irises is worked in long and short stitch with 211.

■ The dark red parts of the poppies are worked in long and short stitch with 498.

■ The bright red parts of the poppies are worked in long and short stitch with 666.

■ The poppy leaves are worked in long and short stitch with 907.

■ The stem is worked in stem stitch with 3346.

■ The yellow parts of the irises are worked in stem stitch with 743.

■ The poppy buds are worked in satin stitch with 666.

■ The iris leaves are worked in satin stitch with 368.

■ The black parts of the poppy centres are worked in French knots with 310.

■ The green parts of the poppy centres are worked in overlapping seed stitches with 368.

12

Thread key

DMC colours used:

- 3740
- 3768
- 503
- 5013
- 3743
- 3042
- 967

Stitches and threads used:

Use 1 strand throughout.

Large paler leaves worked in long and short stitch, inner parts with 503 and outer parts with 5013.

Pale pink flowers worked in long and short stitch, inner parts with 3042 and outer parts with 967.

Small paler leaves and calices worked in long and short stitch in 503.

Small dark leaves worked in long and short stitch with 3768.

Paler side-on flowers worked in long and short stitch with 3743.

The petals of the darker flowers are worked in satin stitch with 3042; pale pink details with 967.

The main stem is worked in satin stitch with 3740.

Pale pink buds are worked in satin stitch with 967.

The outlined calices and leaves are worked in stem stitch with 503.

The pale pink outlined flower parts are worked in stem stitch with 967.

Purple outlined flower parts are worked in stem stitch with 3042.

Brown outlined flower parts and flower details worked in stem stitch with 3740.

Dark green outlined flower parts worked in stem stitch with 3768.

Some centre details worked in French knots with 967 and 3740.

Lines radiating from flower centres worked in straight stitch with 3740.

Dark green centre details worked in lazy daisy stitch with 3768.

13

Thread key

DMC colours used:

- 988
- 470
- 3772
- 760
- 967
- 4190 colour variations
- 945
- 747
- 743

Stitches and threads used for top border:

Use 2 strands throughout.

Paler flowers outlined in stem stitch with 945.

Stem worked in stem stitch with 988.

Pole outlined in stem stitch with 3772.

Large leaves outlined in back stitch with 470.

Small leaves outlined in back stitch with 988.

Pole stripes worked in satin stitch with 4190 colour variations.

Pink flowers outlined in chain stitch with 760.

Lines radiating from flower centres worked in straight stitch with 760 and 945.

Pale blue leaves worked in lazy daisy stitch with 747.

Flower centres worked in French knots with 743.

Stitches and threads used for flower motif:

Use 2 strands throughout.

All lines worked in chain stitch with 945, 967, 988, 3772 and 4190 colour variations.

Flower centres worked in French knots with 743.

Stitch and thread used for bottom border:

Use 2 strands throughout.

All worked in back stitch with 4190 colour variations.

14

Thread key

DMC colours used:

 208

602

 988

4215 colour variations

Stitches and threads used for top border:

Use 2 strands throughout.

Petals, stems and leaves worked in stem stitch with 208 and 988.

Pink flower details worked in lazy daisy stitch with 602.

Stitches and threads used for middle band:

Use 2 strands throughout.

Plain purple petals worked in back stitch with 208.

Other petals worked in back stitch with 4215 colour variations.

Pink details worked in stem stitch with 602.

Stitches and threads used for bottom border:

Use 2 strands throughout.

Flowers, leaves and stems outlined in chain stitch with 208, 602, 988 and 4215 colour variations.

Buds worked in satin stitch with 4215 colour variations.

Centres worked in French knots with 208, 602 and 4215 colour variations.

Thread key

DMC colours used:
- 814
- 223
- 761

Stitches and threads used:

Trunk and branches outlined in stem stitch with 814. Use 1 strand.

Trunk details worked in straight stitch with 814. Use 1 strand.

Leaves outlined in back stitch with 223 and 761. Use 2 strands.

Radiating lines from leaf centres worked in straight stitch with 223 and 761. Use 2 strands.

16

Thread key

DMC colours used:

- 211
- 210
- 209
- 553
- 350
- 3340
- 3341
- 967
- 742
- 743
- 744
- 745
- 772
- 3348
- 471

Stitches and threads used for border:

Use 1 strand throughout.

Orange outlines worked in back stitch with 3340.

Centres worked in French knots with 3340.

Yellow flowers worked in long and short stitch with (from outer to inner parts) 745, 744, 743 and 742.

Lilac flowers worked in long and short stitch with (from outer to inner parts) 211, 210, 209 and 553.

Peach flowers worked in long and short stitch with (from outer to inner parts) 967, 3341, 3340 and 350.

Leaves worked in long and short stitch with (from outer to inner parts) 772, 3348 and 471.

Lines radiating from centres worked in straight stitch with 3340.

Stitches and threads used for flower motif:

Use 1 strand throughout.

Leaves and calyx worked in chain stitch with 3341.

Main flower petals worked in stem stitch with 209.

Stem worked in stem stitch with 471.

Bud and radiating lines from main flower centre worked in stem stitch with 553.

Flower centre worked in stem stitch with 742.

17

Thread key

DMC colours used:

- 937
- 327
- 553
- 209
- 3340
- 3341

Stitches and threads used for bottom border:

Use 2 strands throughout.

Lines worked in chain stitch with 209, 327 and 553.

Hearts filled with satin stitch with 209.

Stitches and threads used for heart motif:

Use 2 strands throughout.

Centre of second flower from bottom outlined in chain stitch and back stitch with 327.

Deep orange inner scalloped edge worked in chain stitch with 3340.

Purple flower centre outlined in chain stitch and back stitch with 3341.

Outer scalloped edge worked in chain stitch with 3341.

Leaves outlined in stem stitch with 937.

Round orange flowers outlined in stem stitch with 3340.

Round flowers' anthers worked in French knots with 937.

Inner purple heart worked in back stitch with 327.

Purple flowers outlined in back stitch with 553.

Lines radiating from flower centres worked in straight stitch with 327, 937 and 3340.

Green flowers outlined in back stitch with 937. Centres in French knots with 3341.

Orange flowers outlined in back stitch with 3340.

18

Thread key

DMC colours used:

	972
	740
	349
	956
	3824
	907
	995

Stitch and thread used for central heart motif:

Use 2 strands throughout.

■ Heart worked in rows of chain stitch with 349.

Stitches and threads used for border:

Use 2 strands throughout.

■■■■■■ Hearts outlined in chain stitch with 349, 740, 907, 956, 972 and 995.

■■ Lines radiating from flower centres worked in straight stitch with 740 and 995.

■■ Flowers outlined in back stitch with 907 and 972.

■■ Details around flower centres worked in lazy daisy stitch with 907 and 956.

■ Line joining border worked in seed stitch with 3824.

19

Thread key

DMC colours used:

■	956
■	349
■	957
■	967
■	470
■	742
■	744
■	E3852 precious metals
■	3819
■	598
■	809
■	210

Stitches and threads used for left-hand border:

Use 2 strands throughout.

■ ■ ■ ■ Large hearts worked in stem stitch, the outer edges in 742 and 956, filled with 744 and 957.

■ Small heart worked in satin stitch with 956.

Stitches and threads used for central heart motif:

Use 2 strands throughout.

■ ■ Flower and leaves worked in back stitch with 349 and 470.

■ Hearts worked in stem stitch with E3852 precious metals.

Stitches and threads used for right-hand border:

Use 2 strands throughout.

■ ■ ■ ■ ■ Large hearts worked in blanket stitch in two interlocking rows with 210, 598, 744, 809, 967 and 3819.

■ Small heart worked in blanket stitch radiating from the centre with 210.

20

Thread key

DMC colours used:

- 4128 colour variations
- E301 light effects

Stitch and thread used for top border:

Use 2 strands throughout.

All worked in back stitch with 4128 colour variations.

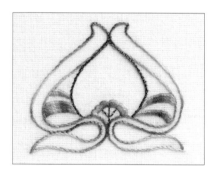

Stitches and threads used for motif:

Use 2 strands throughout.

Outline of outer parts worked in stem stitch with 4128 colour variations.

Brown outlines and details worked in stem stitch with E301 light effects.

Inner shapes filled with satin stitch with 4128 colour variations.

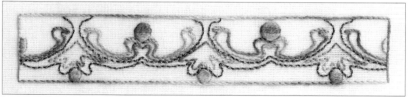

Stitches and threads used for bottom border:

Use 2 strands throughout.

Brown outlines worked in back stitch with E301 light effects. Shapes inside brown outlines worked in back stitch with 4128 colour variations.

Outer border and swirls worked in stem stitch with 4128 colour variations.

Circles worked in satin stitch with 4128 colour variations.

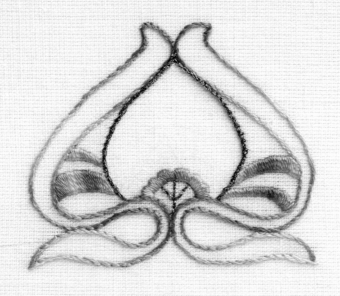

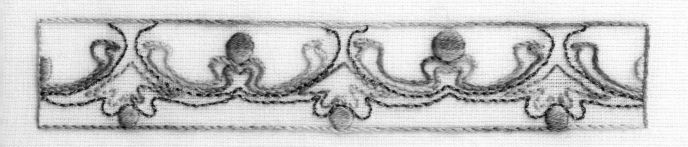

21

Thread key

DMC colours used:

- 4240 colour variations
- E825 light effects
- E3843 light effects
- E334 light effects
- E3845 light effects
- E3849 light effects
- 3819
- 704
- 701
- 906

Stitch and threads used for top border:

Use 2 strands throughout.

All worked in back stitch with 4240 colour variations, E825 light effects and E3845 light effects.

Stitches and threads used for bottom border:

Use 2 strands throughout.

Circles worked in blanket stitch from centres with 3819.

Outer edge worked in stem stitch with 704, 701 and 906.

Swirls worked in chain stitch with 701 and 906.

Stitches and threads used for fish motif:

Use 2 strands.

Main fish outlines worked in stem stitch with E334, E825, E3843 and E3849 light effects.

Fins and tails edged in blanket stitch with E334 and E3845 light effects.

Filled eyes, gills and lips worked in satin stitch with E3843 and E334 light effects.

Use 1 strand.

Straight details worked in straight stitch with E3843 light effects, E3849 light effects and 4240 colour variations.

Scale details worked in lazy daisy stitch with 4240 colour variations.

22

Thread key

DMC colours used:

■ D140 diamant

■ 4126 colour variations

■ D3852 diamant

Stitch and thread used for flower motif:

Use 1 strand of diamant thread.

■ Motif worked in chain stitch with D3852.

Stitches and threads used for border:

■ Flowers and buds worked in back stitch with 2 strands of 4126 colour variations.

■ Stalks and leaves worked in stem stitch with 1 strand of D3852 diamant.

■ Straight edges worked in back stitch with 1 strand of D140 diamant.

23

Thread key

DMC colours used:

- 4210 colour variations
- 3806
- 3837
- 704
- 780

Stitches and threads used for top border and motif:

Use 1 strand of 4210 colour variations throughout.

Leaves worked in blanket stitch.

Trunk, stems and branches worked in back stitch.

Fruits worked in chain stitch.

Stitches and threads used for bottom border and motif:

Use 1 strand throughout.

Leaves worked in blanket stitch with 704.

Trunk, stems and branches worked in back stitch with 780.

Purple fruits worked in chain stitch with 3837.

Pink fruits worked in chain stitch with 3806.

24

Thread key

DMC colour used:

 349

Stitches and thread used:

Use 2 strands of 349 throughout.

Twisted stems and circles in right-hand border and filled petals in central motif worked in satin stitch.

Other filled elements in right-hand border worked in stem stitch.

Bud edges in left-hand border worked in blanket stitch.

Leaves, V-shaped petal edges in central flower motif, loops at bottom of twisted stems and petal edges in right-hand border worked in back stitch.

Radiating lines in buds, flowers and central motif leaves worked in straight stitch.

Edge of flower centre in motif, and flower centres and petal edges in right-hand border worked in chain stitch.

All remaining outlines worked in stem stitch.

Details in flower motif centre worked in French knots.

25

Thread key

DMC colours used:

- 604
- 602
- 351
- 740
- 352
- 741
- 4077 colour variations
- 368
- 3346
- 3045
- 840

Stitches and threads used:

Use 2 strands throughout.

Petals worked in blanket stitch with 4077 colour variations, 740, 741, 602 and 604.

Brown edges of two top sunflowers' centres worked in satin stitch with 840.

Centres filled with French knots with 3045.

Leaves and stems worked in long and short stitch with 352, 351, 368 and 3346.

26

Thread key

DMC colours used:

 349

4200 colour variations

604

Stitches and threads used:

Use 2 strands throughout.

Outline worked in chain stitch in 4200 colour variations.

Spirals worked in back stitch with 349, 604 and 4200 colour variations.

Cross-hatching lines worked in stem stitch with 4200 colour variations.

Cross-hatching filled with seed stitch with 604.

Bands on left-hand side worked in blanket stitch interlocking with 4200 colour variations (top) and 604 (bottom).

Circles at top worked in blanket stitch with 4200 colour variations, 349 and 604.

Four-petal flowers at top left (in rows) and middle right worked in lazy daisy stitch with 349, 604 and 4200 colour variations.

Lines separating patches worked in back stitch with 4200 colour variations.

Attach red and pink buttons of your choice.

Thread key

DMC colours used:

■ 310

▨ 4040 colour variations

Stitches and threads used for square border:

Use 2 strands.

■ Outline worked in stem stitch with 310.

▨ Filling worked in seed stitch with 4040 colour variations.

Stitches and threads used for motif:

■ Outline worked in stem stitch with 2 strands of 310.

▨ Filling worked in back stitch with 6 strands of 4040 colour variations.

Stitch and thread used for bottom border:

▨ All worked in chain stitch with 2 strands of 4040 colour variations.

Thread key

DMC colours used:

■	498
■	3830
■	3350
■	760
■	3810

Stitch and threads used:

Use 2 strands throughout.

■ ■ ■ ■ ■ All worked in back stitch with 760, 498, 3350, 3810 and 3830.

Thread key

DMC colours used:

 666

■ E321 precious metals

■ E3821 precious metals

■ E703 precious metals

■ 987

Stitch and thread used for Christmas tree:

Use 4 strands.

■ Worked in chain stitch with E703 precious metals.

Stitch and threads used for left-hand holly border:

Use 2 strands.

■ ■ All worked in satin stitch with 666 and 987.

Stitch and threads used for star motif:

■ ■ Worked in back stitch with E321 and E3821 precious metals.

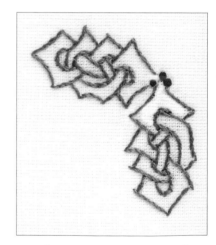

Stitches and threads used for right-hand holly border:

Use 2 strands.

■ Leaves worked in stem stitch with 987.

■ Berries worked in French knots with 666.

30

Thread key

DMC colours used:

E990 fluorescent effects

E980 fluorescent effects

Stitches and thread used for top motif:

All worked with E990 fluorescent effects.
Bubble worked in stem stitch with 2 strands.

Fairy worked in stem stitch with 1 strand.

Flowers worked in lazy daisy stitch with 1 strand.

Stitches and thread used for middle motif:

All worked with E980 fluorescent effects.
Bubbles worked in stem stitch with 2 strands.

Fairy worked in stem stitch with 1 strand.

Flowers worked in lazy daisy stitch with 1 strand.

Stitches and threads used for border:

Use 1 strand of fluorescent effects throughout.

Trailing toadstool stalks worked in back stitch with E990.

Smaller toadstool cap tops worked in back stitch with E980.

Smaller toadstool cap bottoms worked in blanket stitch with E980.

Larger toadstool spots worked in blanket stitch with E990.

Larger toadstool caps outlined in stem stitch with E980.

Smaller toadstool spots worked in satin stitch with E990.

Wider toadstood stalks worked in chain stitch with E990.

31

Thread key

DMC colours used:

- ■ 839
- ■ E321 precious metals
- ■ 51 colour variations
- ■ 107 colour variations
- ■ 666
- ■ 760
- ■ 605
- ■ 819
- ■ E3821 precious metals
- ■ 989
- ■ 121 colour variations
- ■ E852 precious metals

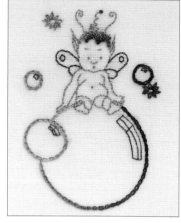

Stitches and threads used for top left-hand motif:

Use 2 strands throughout.

■■■ Fairy worked in back stitch with 989, 51 colour variations and E3821 precious metals.

■ Branch outlined in back stitch and filled with seed stitch with 51 colour variations.

■ Antennae worked in French knots with 989.

■ Flower petals worked in lazy daisy stitch with 51 colour variations.

Stitches and threads used for top right-hand motif:

Use 2 strands unless otherwise stated.

■ Bubbles worked in chain stitch with 121 colour variations.

■ Reflections worked in back stitch with 1 strand of 121 colour variations.

■■ Fairy worked in back stitch with 989 and E852 precious metals.

■ Hair and top of hat worked in French knots with 121 colour variations.

■ Flowers worked in lazy daisy stitch with 121 colour variations.

Stitches and threads used for central motif:

Use 2 strands throughout.

■ Fairy body outlined in chain stitch and filled with lazy daisy stitch with 107 colour variations.

■ Wings worked in back stitch with E321 precious metals.

■ Fairy head worked in back stitch with 989.

■ Petals worked in lazy daisy stitch with E321 precious metals.

■ Spiral worked in back stitch with 107 colour variations.

Stitches and threads used for border:

Use 2 strands throughout.

■ Toadstoods outlined in stem stitch with 839.

■ Larger toadstool caps worked in long and short stitch with 666.

■ Stalks worked in long and short stitch with 819.

■■■ Smaller caps worked in satin stitch in 605, 666 and 760, with spots in white.

■ Tiny toadstool a French knot in 839.

32

Thread key

DMC colours used:

- 4060 colour variations
- 4215 colour variations
- E3837 metals
- 4110 colour variations
- E316 jewel effects
- 963
- 3822
- 402
- E3747 jewel effects

Stitches and threads used for bottom fairy motif:

Use 2 strands throughout.

Wings and antennae worked in stem stitch and French knots with E3837 metals. Wings filled with long and short stitch with 4215 colour variations.

Fairy worked in back stitch with 402. Bubble worked in stem stitch with 4215 colour variations, filled with stem stitch with E3747 jewel effects. Eyes worked in straight stitch with 4215 colour variations and E3837 metals.

Stitches and threads used for central motif:

Use 2 strands throughout.

Wings worked in chain stitch with 4110 colour variations.

Fairy outlined in stem stitch with 402 and E316 jewel effects.

Main flower stem worked in stem stitch with 4110 colour variations; centre in satin stitch with 3822; petals in lazy daisy stitch with 4110 colour variations.

Flower in fairy's hair worked in French knots with E316 jewel effects.

Hair worked in long and short stitch with 3822.

Dress worked in long and short stitch with 963 and 4110 colour variations.

Other flower stems worked in stem stitch with 3822; details in French knots with 4110 colour variations and 3822.

Stitches and threads used for flower motif:

Use 2 strands throughout.

Stems worked in stem stitch in 4060 colour variations.

Centre and leaf worked in satin stitch in 3822 and 4060 colour variations.

Petals worked in lazy daisy stitch with 963 and 4060 colour variations.

Details worked in French knots in 4060 colour variations.

Stitches and threads used for border:

Use 2 strands unless otherwise stated.

Hair and face worked in stem stitch with 1 strand of 963 and 4215 colour variations.

Swirling lines worked in back stitch with 4215 colour variations.

Flowers worked in lazy daisy stitch with 963; centres worked in French knots with 4215 colour variations.

Tiny flowers worked in French knots with 963 and 4215 colour variations.

Eye worked in French knot with 1 strand of 4215 colour variations. Use a blue part.

The projects

The following eight projects are here to inspire you to have a go yourselves. It is important to note that each of these projects was completed in just a couple of evenings. It really doesn't take a lot of time to add a lovely personal touch to an item of clothing or create a keepsake.

When choosing a fabric, try to consider the final use for the stitching. If your work is to be framed, then the choice of fabric is wide open. However, if it is to be a bag or an item of child's clothing, it would be best to use a woven stable fabric such as cotton or a cotton linen mix. Either of these would stand up well to the rigors of use and washing. If you are stitching on a stretchy fabric like a T-shirt or velvet, the fabric will need to be stabilised using some interfacing so that it behaves more like cotton. You can stitch on patterned textiles; just let the shades and design in the fabric guide the final choice of fabric, threads, stitches and colours.

The choice of threads can be great fun; try to think outside the box whenever possible. Take into consideration whether the final piece will need frequent washing and ironing – for instance a tablecloth. In this case, perhaps metallic and fancy threads may not be the best choice. Stranded embroidery cotton will probably always be the first choice, but don't be afraid to experiment stitching with non-traditional threads such as fine wool, crochet cotton or even fine strips of plastic. Using mixed media can be a fast track to a fantastically creative piece of work. For example a very modern design can be produced by overlaying pieces of organza or plastic between your base fabric and decorative stitching.

Bunting

This beautiful summery bunting would cheer up any home or special occasion. The embroidered borders and motifs on the plainer flags complement the more highly patterned fabrics in between perfectly. Note that the gingham makes a good background for embroidery as well as the solid-coloured fabrics.

(See samplers/transfer sheets 8, 18, 4 and 19.)

Baby dress

Here I embroidered a fairy design on to a baby's dress. You could make your own if you like dressmaking, but you could also stitch on a ready-made dress to give it a beautiful personal touch, choosing stitches and threads to complement the garment.

(See sampler/transfer sheet 30.)

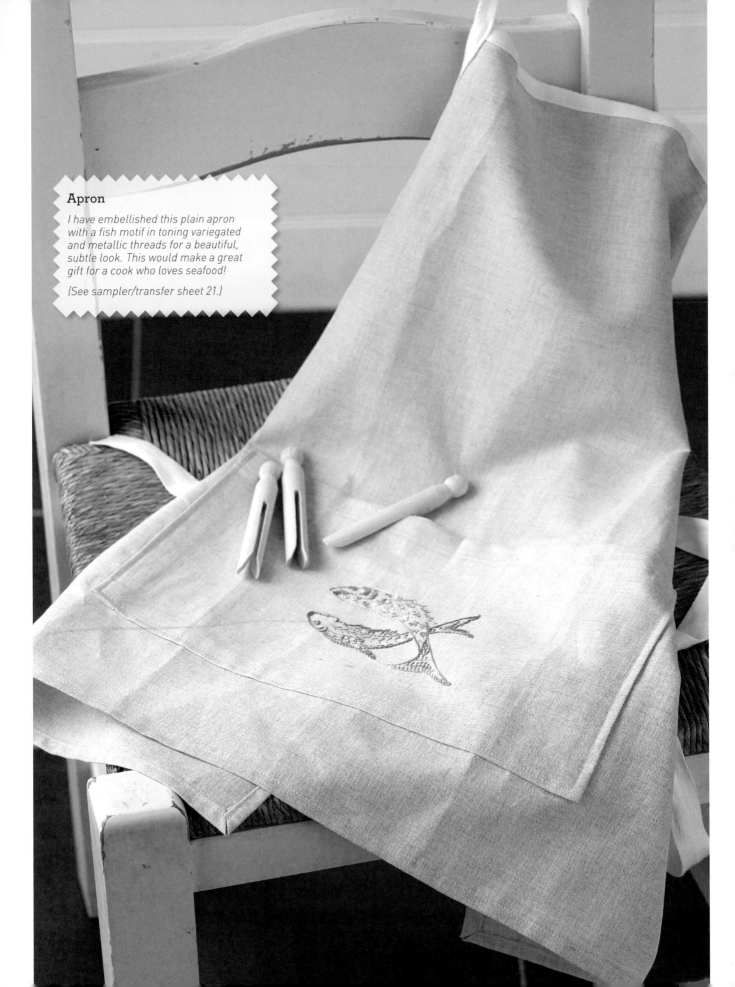

Apron

I have embellished this plain apron with a fish motif in toning variegated and metallic threads for a beautiful, subtle look. This would make a great gift for a cook who loves seafood!

(See sampler/transfer sheet 21.)

Greetings cards

Embroidered motifs make great greetings cards. I stitched these on to crisp white linen and mounted them in plain card blanks that you can buy in craft shops. Try the heart designs in samplers 17, 18, 19 or 26 for Valentine's Day, or make Christmas cards from sampler 29.

(See samplers/transfer sheets 31 and 3.)

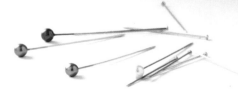

Christmas stockings

Here I have decorated the plain cuffs of these stockings with embroidery to complement the main patterned fabrics, choosing matching and toning threads. Embroiderers have been decorating cuffs with border designs and motifs in this way for centuries.

(See samplers/transfer sheets 29 and 9.)

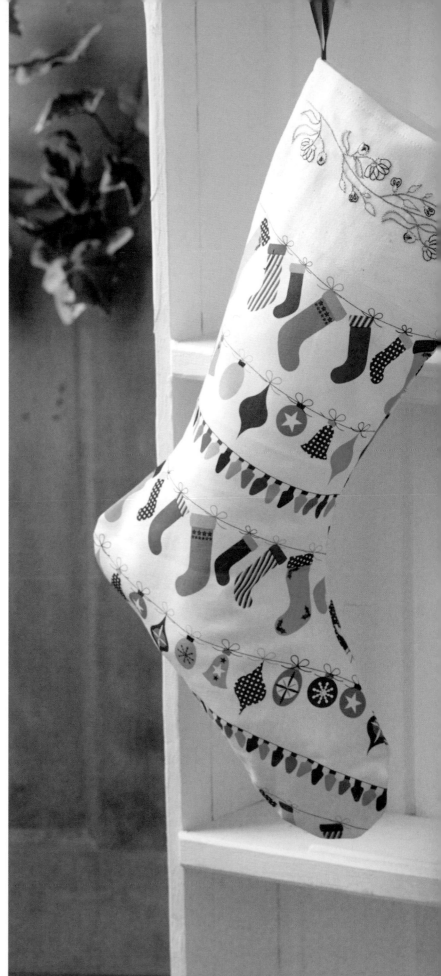

Tote bag

The Japanese maple design gives this plain bag a really modern look. I have chosen bright but natural-looking variegated threads to complement the neutral shade of the bag.

(See sampler/transfer sheet 15.)

Toddler denim set

A border design on the top and a butterfly motif on the shorts bring out the beauty of this little girl's outfit. You could embellish ready-made clothes, transforming them into something really special that can't be bought in the shops.

(See sampler/transfer sheets 14 and 7.)

Bird hangings

These little bird hangings are perfect for embellishing with embroidery and decorating with beads and pendants. Choose your favourite motifs or border patterns from the transfers and create your own flock of beautiful birds.

(See samplers/transfer sheets 3, 14 and 10.)

The transfers

Each of the following transfers corresponds to one of the samplers on pages 16–81 and can be used up to ten times. Once they have been removed from the book by cutting carefully round them with scissors, they can be stored in the pocket on the back cover. Make sure you leave as much paper as possible around the outside.

Note that the ink used on the transfers will fade with washing but may not disappear completely, so when stitching, follow the printed lines as closely as possible to ensure they are hidden beneath the stitching.

3

4

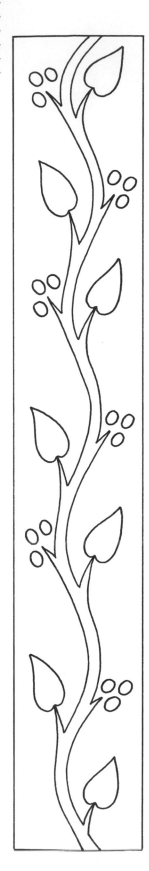

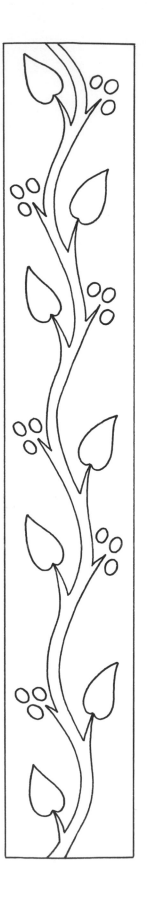

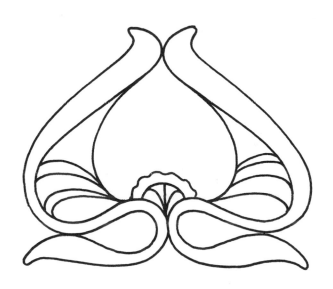

24